"A writer should create living people: people, not characters. A character is a caricature."

Ernest Hemingway

Paula Writes, my blog: paulathewriter.com

Creating Believable Characters

Characters are definitely the most important aspect of any story, for me. Of course, other aspects, such as plot and setting, are also important, but characters are, in my opinion, the heart of fiction.

I tend to approach the development of my fictional people intuitively, and my characters feel like real people already, even when I don't know much about them. I aim to learn more about them, as I go. That's how the process works in real life, after all.

I don't find it beneficial to complete generic character profiles, for the sake of it. To me, this encourages writers to make things up, simply to fill in the boxes - or else, to list, often quite basic and superficial, information, the vast majority of which they know already, such as their main characters' names, ages, and hair colours. If I must write down that my protagonist, Lucy, has red hair, in order to remember something that obvious – to me, that would be worrying.

So, what *does* help your readers to believe in your characters, and start relating to them as real people? Because, after all, it's this level of connection that will make readers care about them – and want to invest their time in reading about them.

Backstory is one vital aspect of creating living, breathing characters. Everyone has a history, including our fictional characters. Consider all aspects of this story – first for major, and then more minor, characters. Think about it, without necessarily writing anything down – at least, initially. If someone is starting to confide in you, but realises that you've been taking notes on them, the whole time, they're going to become more reluctant to open up. Why should characters be any different, in this respect? If you relax, and allow yourself to drift into a kind of daydream, but one which you've entered with specific questions in mind, you're likely to make more progress.

Your characters need to have understandable motivations. Even if they act in ways that you yourself never would, you must feel empathy towards them, and know why they do what they do. Once you understand their motives, you will need to find ways to show this to the reader, during the course of your story.

We all have flaws, and a character who comes across as "perfect" isn't going to be popular with readers. Who is supposed to relate to such a character?

Contradictions, or apparent contradictions, are very real. How many times do you expect someone to do something, and they do the exact opposite? It happens – and should occur with your characters too, from time to time.

Do traits from real people ever find their way into your fiction? If so, that's fine. It's part of what makes characters believable – or it can be. A healthy sign is when it's mixed up, somewhat. One or two traits from a particular real person in any one character is okay, but don't overdo it. If you're anything like me, you will identify aspects of yourself in most, if not all, of your characters – but none should be entirely you, unless you're writing an autobiography, or a memoir.

Everyone approaches writing differently, so perhaps the more generalised character profiles will work for you. But, if these aren't enough, taking the time to delve into your own mind, and those of your characters, could potentially make all the difference.

Naming Your Characters

Choosing character names can be challenging, but it's worth taking the time to consider what names you're giving your fictional people. It can make a more significant difference than many writers assume. The following tips should help.

1. Use baby names websites, such as Nameberry and Behind the Name. There's so much excellent information on these sites, making them invaluable resources for writers.

2. Baby name books can also be useful. As a writer of Modern Historical Fiction, I actually find it a bonus that the name books I own are somewhat out of date.

3. Search online for popular names from specific years, for your own country, or the one in which your story is set. This is, again, particularly relevant for writers of Historical Fiction.

4. Avoid having too many character names that begin with the same letter, or have a similar sound, particularly if those characters are going to appear together in many scenes, throughout the

story. If two names start with the same letter but have a different number of syllables, and don't have a similar sound, it may work. There are twins named Jade and Jessica in my work in progress, and this feels fine to me, but Jade and Jane would be confusing.

5. It can be tempting to simply give characters your favourite names. We all do it. Just don't name all of them as if they were your own children. Presumably, not every character in your novel is supposed to have the same parents, or be from the same background. Try to consider what particular fictional parents might realistically have named their children.

6. For surnames, phone directories or similar lists can be useful. I sometimes take names from the authors on my bookshelves. Non-fiction titles often work best for this. Ensure that first and last names sound right together.

7. Once you have a first and last name combination that feels right to you – and preferably before you have become too attached to it – do a Google search, to ensure that there isn't someone well-known with the same name. We might assume that, if someone was famous, we would have

heard of them, but that isn't necessarily true. Certainly in my own case, I wouldn't have a clue about some of the celebrities out there.

8. Don't overthink the process. Enjoy naming your fictional people, and remember that you can always change the names, at a later date, if any of them don't work out.

Exploring Your Characters' Motivations

It's vital to understand the why behind your characters' actions and reactions – and to communicate this, via your story's events, to the reader.

With the possible exception of minor characters, it's usual for each character to have an arc – a definite pattern of change in that character, from the starting point of the story to the climax. Sometimes the change will be drastic, and sometimes, very subtle, but there will almost always be change, of some description.

Events in real life shape us, and alter our perspectives, and it's the same way for our fictional people. So, in terms of needs and motivations, these will shift and change, as the story moves along.

Your plot will be influenced by the actions and emotions of the various characters, and these actions and emotions can't be understood without knowing what motivates the characters, on multiple levels.

Most people are familiar with Maslow's Hierarchy of Needs, represented by a pyramid. Human needs range from the most basic survival – life or death – needs, to the highest human need, for self-actualisation.

At different times, and in different circumstances, our needs will change. When we're fighting for mere survival, we aren't focusing upon any need higher than that. So, there may be times, in the course of your story, when your characters are fighting for their lives, and at these times, many of their usual priorities, hopes, and dreams, will fade into insignificance.

But there's more to it than this, of course. Desires, goals, dreams – they change over time, even outside of life and death situations. True for all of us, and same applies for our characters. Motivations will be consistent, and yet, evolving, also.

The motivations of one character may be in direct conflict with those of another. This is excellent, from a storytelling perspective, because conflict is essential, in order for your plot to progress, and remain interesting.

The timespan of your story is another consideration. In my own case, my WIP begins in 1983, ending in the early 1990s. My protagonist, Lucy, is seventeen, at the start. The epilogue takes place in 1993. The change between a girl of seventeen, and a twenty-seven year old, who has been through the novel's various events, will obviously be significant. Many of her motivations and needs will be different. These will have changed gradually, over the years, and the challenge is to not only understand these developments ourselves, but communicate them effectively to the reader.

There's so much to say, on the subject of character motivations, and character arcs, and it's difficult to do justice to such a vast, and important, subject. But these are some thoughts on character motivations, which will hopefully be of interest.

Point of View in Fiction: First, Second, or Third Person?

Point of View is an important consideration, when writing fiction. Many of us have favourite points of view, which can become our defaults. This isn't necessarily a problem, as the same point of view may tend to suit most of our writing.

However, it's always worth thinking about the various alternatives, and experimenting with a few of them. All have pros and cons.

First Person

Like many writers, I love, and have often used, first person. My WIP is written in the first person, from the point of view of my protagonist, Lucy. This hasn't been without problems, and I have sometimes wondered how different the novel would be, if I had chosen to write in the third person, and use multiple viewpoint characters. There are specific reasons why I didn't do so, however – and, on balance, I feel happy with the approach I've taken. There's no perfect way in which to tell any story, and there will always be certain compromises.

First person is generally agreed to be the most intimate viewpoint. The writer, and subsequently, readers, are literally inside the mind of the main character, who is referred to by personal pronouns, such as I and me.

However, first person is extremely restrictive. I often struggle with the fact that Lucy has to either be involved directly, or told about, every story event, in order for these to be communicated to the reader. This can be challenging, to say the least.

Multiple viewpoints in first person? Yes, I've seen that done. It's very difficult to pull off, and each character voice needs to be strong and very distinctive. This is always our aim, of course – but it's of even greater importance, if you're going to attempt to use multiple first person narrators. Usually, character names would be used as titles, at the start of chapters or sections, to clarify whose point of view we are in. This seems sensible, to help avoid confusion.

Peripheral narrators are occasionally used, to good effect, in first person novels. An example of this would be The Great Gatsby. The peripheral narrator is someone other than the novel's main character. Although unusual, this technique works, in specific cases, and if you're tempted to take this approach, you probably have a good idea as to why.

Unreliable first person narrators can also be used, and it's worth noting that, to some extent, all first person narrators are unreliable. However, some are unreliable to the extent that we actually refer to them as unreliable narrators, and such characters will have been chosen specifically and strategically by the author. Philip, the first person narrator of du Maurier's My Cousin Rachel, is an example.

Second Person

In second person narratives, the writer uses "you", seeming to address the reader directly. Many people feel uncomfortable with this POV, and find the tone accusatory. I tend to feel this is missing the point. It's equivalent to saying I am literally my main character, Lucy, because I write about her from the first person, saying "I". The use of any POV is a literary device. When used skilfully, any of them can be effective – and that includes second person.

That said, second person is unusual. It can work well in short stories and poetry, and for sections of novels, but entire novels in this POV are rare. It would be extremely challenging to attempt one. Experiment with second person, if it appeals to you, as it's an interesting form, and too easily dismissed.

Third Person

Third person is very popular, and I have written many stories using third person limited. With this POV, characters' names are used in the narrative, and pronouns such as "he", "she", and "they". There are a few variations, when it comes to third person, so we'll look at each of these in turn. Keep in mind, however, that third person limited is the most common.

Third Person Objective

This is basically a "fly on the wall" perspective. The story's narrator doesn't have access to the inner thoughts and feelings of any of the characters. It's an unusual technique, and writing in this POV is certainly interesting, as an exercise. However, attempting to write a novel in third person objective exclusively, would be ambitious.

Third Person Omniscient

Third person omniscient takes things to the opposite extreme. The narrator has access to the thoughts and feelings of every character, and is all-knowing. Again, this isn't an easy perspective to write in. Stories can become messy, confusing, and full of head-hopping. A sense of mystery is almost impossible to maintain.

Third Person Limited

With third person limited, the narrator has access to the thoughts and feelings of certain characters.

Third Person Limited - Single Perspective

In many respects, this is very similar to first person. There are many of the same restrictions and benefits. It can feel slightly less intimate than first person, and at times, slightly less restrictive. In first person, there will be more blending of the author and character voice than in third.

Third Limited - Multiple Perspectives

Third person limited, using multiple perspectives, tends to be the most versatile POV. The number of narrators can range from just two, to many. The more viewpoints used, the more challenging it can be, to keep each voice distinctive, and avoid reader confusion. It's generally advisable to switch perspectives at the end of a chapter - or at least, a section.

Choosing the right POV can sometimes be challenging, but getting it right can make all the difference.

Author Voice and Character Voice

When discussing voice, in connection with writing fiction, we need to distinguish between author voice and character voice.

Author voice refers to the style of the author. This can include word choice and tone. Author voice will be somewhat consistent, although there may be variations between voice used in one work and the next.

Consider your favourite authors, and what it is that appeals to you about their particular writing style. When you read their work, you just know it's that author's work, right? Even if the writer in question writes in multiple genres, there's something that marks each story out as being their own. Daphne du Maurier comes to mind for me, personally.

All writers, then, have a voice, but should you consciously develop that voice? Intentionally focus upon absorbing the styles of other specific authors, so that this will influence your own? Like most other aspects of being a writer, this is an individual choice. Most of us like to at least have some degree of awareness, when it comes to our personal writing styles. But, yes – voice comes naturally, and will develop simply through the fact that we write and read, and live in general.

Character voice is exactly what is says on the tin, as it were. Each character in each story should, ideally, have a clearly defined voice – although it can be challenging to achieve in practice, and a common writing problem is that multiple characters, within a particular story, seem the same, or very similar, in terms of voice.

Character voice is distinct from author voice, although paradoxically, it's also an element of author voice. The extent to which author and character voice merge into one, definitely varies. The general tendency would be for character voice to blend most with author voice in a first person, single viewpoint story. However, this is by no means always the case.

The concept of character voice does tend to refer to viewpoint characters, but it's worth remembering that it applies to other characters, too. But, if a character isn't a POV character, we're going to be relying upon dialogue exclusively, to convey voice.

As I mentioned, author voice does tend to take care of itself, but it can't hurt to be aware of our own developing styles. And, when it comes to character voice - that's definitely an area on which many of us need to focus.

Writing Believable Dialogue

Dialogue is the representation – as opposed to replication – of realistic conversation. By this, I mean that it should sound like real life conversation, to a point – but not entirely. It would be better to consider character dialogue in terms of edited highlights. In reality, people ramble, go off at tangents, and frequently use phrases such as "um" and "er". This is boring to read through, so keep it concise and readable.

As with all aspects of telling a great story, conflict is necessary. Pleasant conversations, where all is happiness and light, and there is no disagreement or problem between your characters, are pointless.   Cut to the drama, wherever possible. Remember that dialogue is a tool, and should be used to move the story forward.

Use dialogue to develop your characters. Differentiate the dialogue of different characters, in as many ways as you can. Consider the range of vocabulary that each character would use – individual word choices. When you actually reach the point of being able to "hear" the characters talking, in your own mind, you will know that you have created real people. Then, you'll know instinctively, if a line of dialogue doesn't fit – because it won't be something this person would actually say, in the particular context.

A major role of dialogue is, as I mentioned, to move the story forward. As such, dialogue is often the perfect place to convey necessary information. However, be careful not to "info dump". Dialogue must sound natural.

And, on the subject of natural sounding dialogue – please take care not to overuse character names.

As in:

"Hello, Mary. How are you today, Mary?"

"Hello, Tom. I'm fine, Tom. How are you, Tom?"

Okay, so it's not normally this bad – but, at times, can come close. Pay attention to real conversations, and you'll realise we don't generally use each other's names that often: mainly at the start of our interactions, or when trying to emphasize a specific point.

Contrary to what you may have been told, said is not dead. It's generally much better than "exclaimed" and the like, which draw attention to themselves, and are principally used for the sake of it, in a misguided effort to keep dialogue "interesting". Some variations, such as "asked" and "yelled", have their place, but "said" is an "invisible" word, and should be your default option. Mix it up with action tags, and instances where no tag is used at all. The latter is more difficult when three or more characters are present, but can be used effectively in dialogue between two characters.

Make use of subtext in your dialogue. It's unrealistic, as well as tedious, for characters to say exactly what they mean, at all times. Multiple layers of meaning add that subtle touch, that will make readers believe in your fictional people and situations.

Writing Romance (Even When You Don't)

I can't advise on writing Category Romance, because I don't. However, relationships in general, are central to all good fiction. This is by no means restricted to romantic relationships, but definitely includes them.

It's also worth noting that many of the most popular love stories, such as Wuthering Heights and Gone With The Wind, don't come under Category Romance. They're love stories, but not Romance, because they don't have happy endings.

Character development is so important, and your romantic story aspects or subplots should ideally be approached with character arcs in mind. One reason why stories of forbidden love are so enduringly popular is because, when done well, they provide an excellent opportunity to explore human psychology. They push characters to their limits, in so many ways.

Consider character backstory. Past experience, when it comes to relationships, will be influential – such as, if your MCs parents, siblings, or close friends, have been through divorce or separation. And, of course, you will need to know about the character's own relationship history. You will also need to know all of this for the MC's love interest. And for any other couples, in the story.

Character flaws are essential – for providing conflict and interest, and creating characters, to whom readers can actually relate. For example, maybe your protagonist, love interest, or both, are prone to jealousy and insecurity. It's easy to imagine how this could lead to potential drama.

Suspense and tension are important in romance, as much so as in other aspects of your plot. There need to be sufficient obstacles, preventing a couple from being together – or else, where is the story?

Romance is not Erotica. Whether or not to include sex scenes is an individual decision, but if the sex, and not the emotion, is the primary focus, then it isn't Romance. And entirely different rules and boundaries apply.

Love triangles. Yes, they're a cliché, but they can and do work. It's a case of ensuring that character development is thorough, and that the plot, as a whole, contains original elements. Use them with caution, but don't feel that they must be avoided, at all costs. This simply isn't true.

Instalove – also known as, love at first sight. This is definitely a cliché, and extremely difficult to write successfully. Instalust, which one or more partner initially believes to be love, is considerably more realistic. Look at it this way. Can you imagine meeting a complete stranger at the local store, and instantly knowing that you were destined to be together eternally, and make babies? And what are the odds that both of you would feel it, and somehow have this connection, out of the blue? The chances of seeing someone you were simply attracted to, and exchanging looks, that could potentially lead to more, if you happened to bump into each other again, multiple times? That is instant mutual attraction, and love can eventually develop from the initial spark. To me, that isn't unrealistic – and it also isn't instalove.

Hopefully, these tips help you to create believable romantic relationships, even if, like myself, you don't write Category Romance.

How To Create Believable Friendships

Fictional friendships are important. How do you ensure that these ring true?

I've already covered romance, but romantic relationships aren't the only type that need attention – in reality, or in our stories.

It's worth considering that, in the context of a story, we will often tend to focus upon maybe one to three close friendships. This is fine. But it's also useful to keep in mind that our main characters will generally have a wider friendship circle, of some description. It can sometimes be beneficial to include a name or reference here and there, in order to reflect this.

When developing a friendship, consider the backstory – the history behind the friendship. My main character, Lucy, has been best friends with Charlotte since primary school. As well as going to school together, they used to be neighbours. This does mean that they have a great deal of shared history. Yet, they have also grown apart, in many respects. By the end of the novel, Charlotte isn't Lucy's exclusive "best friend", in quite the same way. At the same time, that shared history will always be there – and that would be the case, even if the friendship ended.

Think about the why behind the friendship. There are usually multiple reasons. In the case of Lucy and Charlotte, obviously they would have become friends partly due to circumstances – because they lived so close to each other and went to school together. So, yes - the met at school, through work, or at the local chess club, part is always going to be there. But then there will be other factors, including shared interests, shared secrets, a similar sense of humour – or, going deeper, the same core values. Maybe the friends are actually opposites, in many respects? Which can be good or bad – or a bit of both.

All friendships have their ups and downs, and this definitely needs to be reflected. In some stories, it will a major plot point or a subplot – but, even if it isn't, it should ideally be communicated, to some degree. No friendship is perfect, after all. The problems and misunderstandings are part of what makes the relationship feel realistic. In this way, hopefully, your reader will be able to relate, and being able to relate leads to caring.

Make sure that your friend characters are fully developed in themselves, and not simply "sidekicks", with no other obvious role in life. They need to have their own lives, and not everything they do will be about their friend, even if said friend happens to be your protagonist.

Hopefully, these tips will help you to create believable friendships in your fiction. You might even start to envy your fictional characters, for having such strong friendships. That's a good sign, because it shows that you believe in your own characters, and can feel the strength of their friendship.

Killing Off Characters

So, time to discuss death: Character death, that is. Here are 10 points to consider, when it comes to killing off your fictional people.

Whether you love or hate this aspect of storytelling, it's something that we have to deal with, as writers: that sometimes our "babies" need to die. This will probably sound disturbing to non-writers, but most of us, to some extent, find it therapeutic, to commit "murder", on the page.

1. The genre and type of story are factors. The number, and nature, of character deaths, will be influenced by category and genre, as well as your own personal preferences and style. If you have a specific target audience in mind, then think about their needs and preferences. Scenes of extreme graphic violence would generally be deemed unacceptable, in the context of Children's or YA Fiction. Even within Adult Fiction, there are going to be variations. A Romance or Women's Fiction novel would generally not be littered with fictional corpses. If you're venturing into the territory of Horror, dark Thrillers, or Crime, it could be time to bring on those dead bodies.

2. The death of a character - or characters - should advance the plot. It ought to move the story forward, in one or more respects. If it doesn't do that, you need to seriously question whether the death is necessary. It may be that it motivates other characters, thus becoming a catalyst for future events. Often, you'll be able to come up multiple story benefits to a single character death, in which case, you'll know you're on the right track.

3. Death can create a sense of realism. This, combined with advancing the plot, is a good reason to kill a character. If you're writing about drug addiction and the criminal underworld, it wouldn't be unexpected for some of your characters to die.

4. Death can sometimes be used to drive home a point, emphasizing the work's central theme. This could certainly tie in with my last example, about drug addiction.

5. Avoid killing characters for the shock factor alone. If the only point of the death is to horrify the reader, don't do it. No-one is going to be impressed.

6. You'll sometimes realise you've included an unnecessary character. In this situation, many writers feel tempted to kill off said character. Almost certainly, not the best solution. The truth is, there is no easy fix. If the character never had a significant role in the story, it's a case of going back, and reworking all scenes in which that character appears. In other words, delete them. It's called editing, right? It has to be worth the extra effort.

7. How about characters who are literally created to die? No problem, as far as I'm concerned. In fact, if you're a plotter, as I am, then the aim is to know, in advance, which characters are going to die. Now, in my own case, this does alter, as I write. I'm not a "synopsis set in stone" writer, even though I do start with an outline. I tend to end up with more character deaths than I started out with, rather than the other way around. But, anyway - the "born to die" characters are ones whose primary purpose, in the story, literally is to end up dead. As long as the reason for the demise meets the criteria mentioned thus far, there's absolutely nothing wrong with inventing characters for the purpose of killing them.

8. Research is vital. Whether a character is stabbed or poisoned, involved in a road traffic accident, or

dies of a heart attack, or a form or Cancer, it's important to get the facts right. With the internet at our disposal – in addition to more traditional research methods, such as reading books, and talking in person to experts - it's easier than it's ever been. Still hard work, but in comparative terms, straightforward – and part of the job, in my opinion.

9. As with other areas of writing, avoid cliché. You only have to consider a handful of TV dramas, and some cliché death scenes should come to mind. These will jolt your reader out of the story, shattering the illusion, and making it feel fake. So much for the deep emotions that you might otherwise have stirred.

10. Finally, remember that death is followed by grief. You can choose to leap into the future, skipping the intense mourning period, which is legitimate. Even then, however, you have to address the issue of ongoing grief, for the characters who remain. The process is not linear. Everyone goes through grief in real life, and if you truly love your characters, and they feel like real people to you, you will not shy away from addressing their grief, when people they love die. Allow yourself to feel

their pain, and then hopefully, your readers will, too. We aim to break our readers' hearts, after all.

Paula Writes, my blog: paulathewriter.com

twitter.com/paulapuddephatt

instagram.com/paulamichellepuddephatt

pinterest.co.uk/paulapuddephatt

facebook.com/paulaperceptions

facebook.com/paulapoems

paulapuddephatt.tumblr.com